The Women's Suffrage Movement

Meghan Cooper

Cavendish Square
New York

Library of Congress Cataloging-in-Publication Data

Names: Cooper, Meghan, author.
Title: The women's suffrage movement / Meghan Cooper.
Description: New York : Cavendish Square Publishing, 2018. |
Series: The interwar years | Includes bibliographical references and index.
Identifiers: LCCN 2016055206 (print) | LCCN 2016057659 (ebook) |
ISBN 9781502627117 (library bound) | ISBN 9781502627124 (E-book)
Subjects: LCSH: Women--Suffrage--United States--History--Juvenile literature. | Suffragists--United States-
-Biography--Juvenile literature. | Women--Political activity--United States--Juvenile literature.
Classification: LCC JK1898 .C66 2018 (print) | LCC JK1898 (ebook) | DDC 324.6/230973--dc23
LC record available at https://lccn.loc.gov/2016055206

Editorial Director: David McNamara
Editor: Kristen Susienka
Copy Editor: Alex Tessman
Associate Art Director: Amy Greenan
Designer: Alan Sliwinski
Production Coordinator: Karol Szymczuk
Photo Research: J8 Media

Contents

INTRODUCTION

Before Women Could Vote

T he world is constantly changing. In the past two hundred years, this change has been more explosive than many of our ancestors could have dreamed. We have seen the major mode of transportation go from the horse-drawn carriage to the gasoline-powered car, and world travel progress from slow-moving ships to superfast airplanes. We have gone from open fires to heat and light our homes to efficient natural gas and hydroelectric plants that provide electricity and heat with the flick of a switch. Communication, formerly carried out by letters sent on horseback, is more efficient than ever with cellular phones and email. We have seen books progress from hand-printed and hand-bound to mass-produced, before being made available on electronic handheld devices. Knowledge has moved from elite libraries

Opposite: A Puritan woman reads a book while spinning yarn, a common household duty for women of her time.

to the most stunning invention of all, the internet—right at our very fingertips.

Rights for Women

While today it is hard to imagine what life was like before these wonderful innovations, it may be harder still to imagine what life was like before women were US citizens, considered equal to men. While laws now protect women from being fired from a job for being pregnant or being banned from college based only on their sex, there was a time not so long ago when women had almost no rights at all. Women could not walk the streets alone or participate in public life. They could not own property, attend most schools, divorce their husbands no matter how brutally they were treated, and they certainly could not vote. Women who were enslaved or were people of color had even fewer rights.

The Role of Women

For much of the nineteenth century, women were considered to be born to the role of wife and mother, and were not allowed to venture out of a domestic life. This was not just a societal expectation, though it was strongly reinforced by the etiquette of the day. It was also backed by a dubious science that claimed women were, by their very natures, too emotional for most jobs. They were thought to be too delicate to do manual labor, and so intellectually inferior to men that they could not participate in politics or law. Due to the belief that women were not intellectually capable of managing their own finances, all of a wife's property belonged to her husband, including any wages she earned from working outside the home. If her husband divorced her, he was automatically granted custody of their children.

A woman's place was in her home, and her job was caring for the house and children. In the time before modern conveniences, this was hard work, indeed. Women's tasks might include carrying water to the house from a stream or well for cleaning, cooking, and drinking. They were expected to keep their homes clean and scrubbed, which often required making their own supplies. Brooms, polishes, and cleaning solutions were usually made at home. Women did the wash and the ironing, prepared meals from scratch, canned and preserved food for the winter, sewed and mended the family clothes, cared for the children, and made quilts, candles, and other household necessities. If they lived on a farm, they also assisted with the chores, such as milking the cows, feeding the chickens and collecting the eggs, and churning the milk into butter. They were expected to be charming and entertain guests in their home, and to cater to the needs of the family without ever questioning their husbands' opinions. In essence, women were expected to make themselves subservient to their husbands. Despite all this work, women were considered a physically weaker sex, less capable than their male counterparts.

Women often helped with chores around the farm in addition to caring for the household. Here, a woman helps her husband shear sheep.

At this time, women were also less likely to take jobs outside the home than men, although poor women and women of color often held jobs. Usually, such professions involved domestic labor. Women worked as seamstresses, provided childcare, or became domestic servants, where they earned very low wages. It was believed that women did not need to make as much money as men because, unlike men, women were not expected to support a household financially. This was problematic for women who were the sole breadwinners due to extenuating circumstances. Women who taught school—one of few acceptable professions for literate women—only earned about a quarter of what a male teacher made. They were often fired from their posts if they became engaged or married. Some women worked as shopkeepers, tailors, or silversmiths, or sold baked goods or dairy products from their homes. These jobs were in addition to caring for their homes and children. Even when women worked outside the home, it was never considered to be a man's job to step in and help with household chores.

Accessing Education

Women who did take jobs outside the home were limited in their options, both because of the belief that women could not properly fill most roles of employment, but also because access to education was limited. Most girls only received a grammar school education at best, because the most important thing that they were expected to learn was homemaking. A girl only needed to be able to capably cook, clean, and provide a home for her husband and children, so studying mathematics and science seemed a waste of time. Women were discouraged from public speaking and expressing themselves through writing, so teaching them to read or write beyond a basic level was not deemed important. Even when girls became students of history, there were few historical representations of women in literature or history for them to connect to.

Wealthier families might opt to send their daughters to private high schools, called "academies," but families with smaller incomes often could not justify the expense of sending a girl to school, knowing she would likely end up a mother and a wife without the option of pursuing a career. While high school was not compulsory for males or females, many

The first co-educational high schools often had more male students than female. The women who did graduate had limited options after graduation.

oppression. Women such as Elizabeth Cady Stanton, Lucretia Mott, Susan B. Anthony, and Lydia Maria Child worked tirelessly to voice their opinions and strove for the rights of slaves as well as women everywhere. Unfortunately, many would not live to see their efforts grow to fruition, but they would certainly inspire future generations.

The Civil War

The Civil War was a time of deep division. However, it was also an episode of American history that introduced women to new roles. Many women during this time focused their energy on aiding the troops, either through aid societies, **petitions**, or pursuits closer to the battlefield. The first women's political organization in the country, the Women's Loyal National League (WLNL), was founded by women's rights **activists** during the Civil War. This organization fought for passage of the Thirteenth Amendment to the US constitution. They gathered a significant number of signatures (four hundred thousand) on a petition to abolish slavery and presented it to Congress. It was, at that time, one of the largest petitions in the history of the United States. This allowed women a socially appropriate way to become involved in politics without directly challenging the social norms.

It would be one hundred years before women could enlist in the military, but hundreds of women disguised themselves as men (400 Union, 250 Confederate) and went into battle during the Civil War. Since women were assumed to be less

WOMEN'S EMANCIPATION PETITION.

☞ Put no signatures on the back of the Petition.
☞ When this sheet is full, paste another at the bottom.
☞ If possible, send us contributions to help pay the heavy expenses incurred at this office.
☞ Do not copy the names—return the original signatures; no matter if the paper is worn or soiled.
☞ When your district is thoroughly canvassed, return the petitions and donations to this office.
☞ Address Susan B. Anthony, Secretary, W. N. L. National League, Room 20, Cooper Institute, New York.

To the Senate and House of Representatives of the United States :

The Undersigned, Women of the United States above the age of eighteen years, earnestly pray that your Honorable Body will pass, at the earliest practicable day, an Act emancipating all persons of African descent held to involuntary service or labor in the United States.

NAME.	RESIDENCE.
Eliza Williams	Seneca Nemeha Co Kansas
Rhoda M. Mudeolf	Ourcaouk Nemaha Co Kansas
Ellen Lewis	
Lyyia S. Fuller	Seneca Neosh Co Ka
N. C. Fuller	" "
H. A. Stower	"
Lyyie N. Fulton	" "
Mary A. Burnes	" "
Amanda M. Lashin	" "

Like many suffrage groups at the time, the Women's Loyal National League used petitions, like this one, to try and enact legal and social change for women.

intelligent, and this made them generally less suspicious than any man, women made perfect spies during this time. They often gained access to enemy plans by acting flirtatiously to get enemy soldiers to speak about upcoming deployments or attacks. Many others, such as Clara Barton, founder of the American Red Cross, went to the front as nurses and aided soldiers wounded on the battlefield. Barton was quoted as saying that the Civil War caused "fifty years in the advance of the normal position" of women, due to the new opportunities suddenly afforded them in wartime.

Women also had to take over many of the roles of men in household duties and in local jobs, as the majority of the men went to war. This had a dramatic effect on the concept of gender roles, as women were suddenly proving themselves far stronger and far more competent than they were previously considered. Women were experiencing freedom to pursue their own interests, care for themselves, manage their own finances, and pursue roles other than wife and mother.

Expanding America

After the Civil War, in the 1870s, America experienced a time of unmatched prosperity and an economic boom. Railroads were being built to connect the ever-growing country, banking and finance institutions flourished, and coal mining and steel manufacture benefitted from new advances in machinery and the ability to transport cargo freely around the country. Advances in machinery also helped American farms grow and become more profitable.

While these opportunities allowed for economic prosperity, there was an unfortunate side effect: a system of corruption in the United States government. Business tycoons often paid their way into political positions or used their wealth and influence to force politicians to bow to the demands of the growing economy. The laws that resulted from these bribes usually benefitted industry and those in power, while hurting the workers and the common man. This prosperity was also dubious, as it did not extend to women or people of color.

Discontent with political circumstances increased, and many more women began to see education, legal rights, and **enfranchisement** as answers to the helplessness they felt when faced with a political climate they had no control over. Women joined women's organizations and political groups in hopes of enacting societal change. Many felt that the right to vote would help women make decisions in society, and **suffrage** groups gained momentum.

World War I

When World War I began in 1914, then-president Woodrow Wilson adhered to a **laissez faire** foreign policy campaign, hoping to keep the United States out of the conflict. But he could not avoid it forever. His position became more precarious after German torpedoes sank the British liner RMS *Lusitania*, killing 128 Americans onboard. Nevertheless, Wilson continued the policy of noninvolvement but warned Germany that America would be forced to fight if it continued to attack ships carrying US passengers. In 1917, Germany did just that. They began to launch massive torpedo attacks on American merchant ships, and on April 2, 1917, the United States joined the war.

Wilson believed that the only way to win the war was with massive manpower, so he implemented a **draft**, forcing most men of eligible age to go. Altogether, 2.8 million US men would fight overseas.

Just as during the Civil War, women were thrust into the public sphere. Many went overseas to serve as nurses, but others went as clerks, scribes, or telephone operators. This left important roles to be filled at home. Once more, women assumed traditionally men's professions, but this time the world was a different place. By World War I, the American way of life had shifted as a result of industrialization. More factories had been set up, and more industries were created. Women went to work in these factories, or as police officers and postmasters, and once again took over the financial responsibilities of their husbands and fathers. However, when the men returned, women were not willing to give up their new rights. The push for suffrage was stronger than ever because of the new roles afforded by World War I.

In the years that followed, significant events would affect women in the United States—the most important of which was attaining women's suffrage in 1920, a feat that took great strength and sacrifice to accomplish.

The World Is Changing

By the end of World War I, a new kind of sentiment had arisen in the United States. Many women around the country considered themselves valuable contributors to society and pushed for equality, especially the right to vote. They launched a campaign that became known as the women's suffrage movement. It would affect many, face many challenges, and forever change the way women were viewed in America.

To achieve that aim, however, many others had to first set the groundwork. The women's suffrage movement of the 1910s built upon the foundations laid by the first human rights and social improvement campaigns of the 1850s, among them the **abolitionist movement** and the **temperance movement**.

Opposite: *The World Anti-Slavery Convention of 1840 largely disregarded the contributions of women to the abolitionist movement.*

The Abolition Movement

Many women who would later become the most prominent figures in the suffrage movement were first inspired by abolitionists. Abolitionism, or the abolitionist movement, aimed to end slavery in all the states in the Union, and provided aid to slaves in their fight for freedom. Abolitionists were largely social reformers who believed that slavery was a violation of human rights, or evangelical Christians who considered slavery a moral abhorrence and a national sin. Many abolitionists were white Northerners and free African American people, who helped organize systems like the Underground Railroad to free slaves. Among them were Elizabeth Cady Stanton, Frederick Douglass, Susan B. Anthony, Sojourner Truth, and Lucretia Mott.

While abolitionists all agreed on ending slavery, the approaches to do so often varied widely. Some called for a gradual reduction in slave ownership with the ultimate goal of abolishing the practice. Others wanted the immediate release of all slaves. Some abolitionists believed that slaves should gain full equal rights in the United States once emancipated, while others thought that after being freed, African American people should have fewer rights than their white counterparts.

In the years leading up to the Civil War, most European countries had banned slavery. The Northern states had mostly abolished slavery by the early 1800s, while nearly all of the Southern states still allowed for it and the slave trade. Abolitionists were met with strong contention from Southern slave owners, as well as Northerners who believed that challenging the social order would lead to the downfall of the Union. Plantation owners believed that they would fail economically if they were forced to employ laborers at a fair wage rather than keep a staff of unpaid labor on their large plantations and farms.

Arguments for the continued ownership of slaves included many of the arguments against women being included in political systems: they were believed to be mentally inferior, unable to care for themselves, and in need of supervision. As with the denial of rights for women, religious institutions and religious tradition often used biblical passages to justify enslavement. White men tended to use rhetoric that implied it was hard work caring for the women and slaves in their lives, insisting both groups should be grateful instead of fighting for equal rights.

The Temperance Movement

One of the movements that had the greatest crossover with the early women's rights movement was the temperance movement. Temperance is the idea that all alcohol should be strictly limited or banned, even to the point of complete legal **prohibition**. In the early 1800s, there was a push by some groups to eliminate all alcohol sale and consumption in the United States—and many temperance supporters were women.

THE QUAKERS

Among the earliest voices calling for an end to human slavery were the **Quakers**. This religious group, also called the Society of Friends, was founded in England in the 1700s. In the early colonial days, they traveled to America mainly as missionaries but also to escape religious persecution. Once in America, however, they found themselves persecuted by Puritans. These hardships did not deter them, though. Quakers still managed to foster growing communities in Rhode Island, New Jersey, and Pennsylvania, and would heavily influence the politics in those regions.

Unlike other evangelical Christian sects, the Quakers believed that God lives within each person and rejected ideas of hierarchy and vanity. Quakers also believed that every person was equal in God's eyes, and that women and all races should be treated equally by laws and by one another to reflect the goodness of God in each person. They abstained from alcohol, wore plain clothes, and fought against societal inequalities.

Many Quakers would become entrenched in politics over the course of history, fighting for equality. Prior to and during the Civil War, they were instrumental in the formation of the Underground Railroad, taking leadership roles and using their own houses to hide escaped slaves. They were known for their prowess in public speaking, and many great speakers of the time were Quakers. This list included Lucretia Mott, one of the founders of the early women's suffrage movement and the keynote speaker at the first women's rights convention in America in 1848.

The American Temperance Society

The American Temperance Society was formed in 1826, and by 1835 it had 1.5 million members, about half of whom were women. This was unusual for the time, since most organizations did not allow female members. In 1869, social issues like temperance often took a backseat to more pressing, postwar-related issues, but that year, the National Prohibition Party formed. They focused on prohibition and social conservatism, and are the oldest third party in America that still operates today. From their inception, they allowed women to be party members, and they were the first **political party** to do so. Not only were women allowed to join, but they were given full delegate rights at party conventions. In an unprecedented move, women National Prohibition Party members could argue the platform and discuss ideology and party ideals alongside men. They added suffrage to their party platform as early as 1872, and equal pay for women by 1892.

The Women's Christian Temperance Union

What started out as the women's branch of the National Prohibition Party would eventually become the Women's Christian Temperance Union (WCTU), one of the most influential groups in both the temperance and the suffrage movements. They were founded in 1873 and had become the biggest organization of women in the world by 1890. Under the leadership of their second president, noted feminist

Frances Willard, they adopted a policy of "do anything." This meant they would fight for any cause they found important, instead of focusing just on prohibition. These other ideals included women's suffrage, child labor laws, education reform, prison reform, and world peace.

Women widely supported temperance because they saw it as a way to make sure finances weren't squandered by a drunk husband at a saloon. Considered hotbeds of contention, corruption, and dirty dealings, saloons were places that promoted drinking and could easily prompt a man to spend all his money, leaving none for his family. Additionally, as women had few rights after a divorce, it was often financially and legally impossible to leave a man who was abusive to his wife and children while in drunken rages. The WCTU advocated for women with husbands who suffered from alcoholism at a time when women were underrepresented legally, banned from politics, and prevented from voting to enact legal changes.

However, that was not all. The WCTU was also instrumental in the **ratification** of the Eighteenth Amendment in 1919, which banned the purchase and sale of liquor in the United States until the amendment was repealed in 1933.

An Issue with Saloons

Frances Willard guided the WCTU to make changes through education, but there were more **radical** members of the temperance union that took more dangerous approaches to enact change. One example is Carrie Nation, who gained

Carrie Nation stands with her iconic axe.

notoriety for her use of hatchets and other blunt objects to demolish bars. Nation had been briefly married to an alcoholic, and believed that she had been chosen by God to lead the temperance movement in a more visual and violent direction after the marriage dissolved. She led groups of women, all armed with weapons, in raids against saloons. There they would smash bottles of alcohol, chop tables and chairs in two, and threaten the saloonkeepers with violence if they intervened.

The Progressive Era

From the end of the Civil War until World War I, the political climate in the United States was shifting considerably. The 1870s had been a time of lavish growth and economic prosperity, but soon people began to resent the outright corruption of their elected officials, and the corporations forming giant monopolies that drove smaller companies out of business. This disgust fueled what would be known as the **Progressive Movement**, or the Progressive Era.

Beginning in the late 1890s, the United States found itself in a state of social and political upheaval. Social activism and political reform brought government corruption to the forefront of the American public's awareness. Several ideals were at the heart of the Progressive Movement: race and gender inequity, anti-trust laws and big business, temperance, education, labor, and women's rights. As progressives fought to modernize the United States and incorporate scientific and engineering discoveries into politics, they were naturally drawn to a theoretical advancement now known as **Taylorism**. Taylorism is a theory of management that examines and integrates workflows using the scientific method, with a focus on creating efficiency. Fred W. Taylor and his followers believed that by studying a task and how it is completed, they could determine the "one true way" to complete each task. The adoption of this theory led to reorganization within public education, medicine, finance, economics, industry, and conservation. It also gained hold in US business and even in the home, causing people to look for new and innovative ways to accomplish everyday activities.

Around 1900, with the expansion and efficiency of printing presses and the added financial backing publications received from advertising, magazines become popular in American culture. Initially somewhat expensive in the 1800s, in the 1900s, magazine cover prices fell to roughly 10 cents an issue, making them highly desirable and very affordable. Groups used magazines to promote progressive ideas among their readership.

Likewise, journalism began to develop different angles. **Muckrakers** used investigative journalism to expose corruption and bring public awareness to social issues like child labor, poverty, and women's rights. This was a field that men continued to dominate, but women were increasingly accepted. Ida Tarbell, a famous muckraker, received notoriety after she targeted the Rockefellers and their Standard Oil Trust monopoly in her article, "The History of the Standard

Oil Company," published in *McClure's Magazine*. Her reporting helped break up that infamous monopoly.

African American issues were largely ignored by progressives, and many viewed racial inequality as a natural force or unimportant crusade. However, there were a few notable exceptions. Mary White Ovington and Oswald Garrison Villard organized the National Association for the Advancement of Colored People (NAACP) during the Progressive Era, and brought the racism that many African Americans endured to the awareness of the American public. Another example was Ida B. Wells, an African American schoolteacher who sued a railroad company after being forced to get off a train when she wouldn't give her seat to a white person. She fought against racial discrimination and lynching by publishing scathing articles condemning racism and violence. She was also a leader in the suffrage movement for African American women.

Labor Unions

For much of the nineteenth century and early twentieth century, businesses could mistreat their employees without legal recourse. There were no legal constraints on how employers treated their employees: no minimum wage, no minimum working hours, no restrictions on workplace safety, and no requirements to provide breaks or benefits to employees. People were often abused by their employers—locked into their workrooms at factories, forced to work excruciatingly long hours, or paid less than the agreed-upon wage. Conditions were terrible. Taking the fight into their own hands, workers began to form organizations that would advocate for their rights. These were called unions.

Labor unions functioned as bargaining collectives for workers to demand fair pay and other workplace measures that promoted well-being. Union members pressured bosses through petitions, promoting political candidates who fought for workers' rights, and conducting work strikes, during which time they would prevent other workers from taking their places in factories by forming picket lines.

The labor movement was a big part of enacting child labor laws in the United States. The Working Men's Party and the American Federation of Workers fought for laws against the use of child labor. Children were often employed in factories because they could be paid very little. The pressure from these two groups motivated legislators in the United States to pass laws requiring a minimum working age in 1904.

The Food and Drug Administration

Another progressive achievement was the Food and Drug Administration (FDA), which formed in 1906 to ensure purity of food and drink for families. Prior to this, food was sold without much thought to the safety of the contents. This meant meat might be tainted with tuberculosis, or food would sit on shelves without proper handling instructions or expiration dates. Clean water was not always available to people for drinking, and public water supplies were not tested for toxins. The FDA changed this by setting limits on food

THE TRIANGLE SHIRTWAIST FACTORY FIRE

On March 25, 1911, a fire broke out in the Triangle Factory, which occupied the top three floors of the Asch building in New York City. Firefighters believed that a match or cigarette butt started the fire, but in the cramped factory, full of scraps of leftover fabric that had not been disposed of, the fire quickly spread.

As the fire escalated, people flocked to the exits, the lone working elevator, and the roof. However, the raging flames and smoke blocked one of the building's main stairwells. A door leading to a second stairwell had been locked previously to prevent theft or unauthorized cigarette breaks. People who tried to escape through these areas were burned alive. Then the elevator stopped working. It had been overcome by the heat of the blaze. The remaining workers in the factory were trapped. Some tried to leap to safety through the elevator shaft. Others attempted to crawl down the fire escape. However, it broke away from its bearings and spilled at least twenty people onto the street below, killing them.

Many workers had nowhere else to go except to the street by way of jumping. Others who could not bear that demise succumbed to the smoke or flames.

While firefighters arrived quickly, their ladders would not reach the top floors, and the accumulation of bodies on the ground made it difficult to get to the building. The safety nets they held out for people tore under the weight of the bodies, and were of little use. It was a horrific end for many young workers. In total, 145 people—mostly young immigrant women—were tragically killed that day.

The horror of this incident shook the American people and led to reforms in workplace safety as well as legislation to prevent future horrors. Today it is remembered as one of the deadliest industrial incidents in US history.

A scene from the Triangle Shirtwaist Factory Fire

and water safety and legally enforcing those laws. They began to discredit "medicines" sold to the public with crazy claims of cures without any scientific evidence that the drugs were helpful. The FDA still exists today, with rigorous standards for food, water, and pharmaceutical safety.

Women's Clubs

Another organization stemming from the progressive movement was the General Federation of Women's Clubs (GFWC) in 1890. The group united more than sixty women's clubs nationally. Many of these clubs began as book clubs or writer's circles, but they also represented philanthropy, civic responsibility, and volunteer efforts by women across the country. Likewise, many were devoted to suffrage.

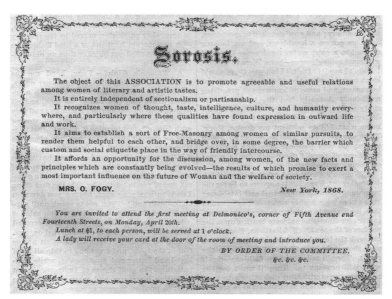

Here is an advertisement for the first meeting of the Sorosis Club, generally considered the first professional women's club in the United States.

The GFWC represented different regions with very different ideals. Because of these differences, the clubs had problems with members fighting about race (there were attempts to block African American women's groups from joining, for instance). Despite these setbacks, the GFWC became the major outlet for women's voices prior to the ratification of the **Nineteenth Amendment**.

World War I and the Draft

During World War I, with men fighting on the front in Europe, women were suddenly thrust into a new role in daily life. Some held jobs as schoolteachers or domestic servants, but during World War I, other professions became available to them. Some women served as nurses, worked in munitions factories, and even served as police officers and worked in post offices. Women also took over family farms in the absence of the men, making sure daily chores of feeding and milking animals, harvesting and planting crops, and slaughtering animals were done. There were women who went to Europe as well, serving in the war as nurses, cooks, and telephone operators.

At this point in history, more women than ever were working outside the home and gaining their own financial and social independence. This freedom pushed women toward gaining the right to vote, because enfranchisement would mean the continued ability to live and work outside of the home with safe conditions while being represented by people who had their best interests in mind.

A woman works in a munitions factory during World War I.

International Suffrage

The United States wasn't the only country fighting for women's suffrage. Internationally, women's rights issues were coming to the forefront in many nations throughout the nineteenth and twentieth centuries. In 1881, the Isle of Man gave women who owned land or property the right to vote, while another British colony, New Zealand, gave all women the right to vote in 1893. Some Australian colonies had limited voting rights prior to 1902, but when the six Australian colonies (then under British rule) combined that year, all women (except aboriginal women) were granted suffrage.

A few European countries, including the grand dutchy of Finland, a part of the Russian empire, gave women full voting rights and even elected the world's first female members of Parliament in 1907, followed by Norway in 1913. But still, globally, women had fewer rights than men.

In the United States, life after World War I became a time of increasing independence. Many people saw the war as a way to spread American democracy to other parts of the world, but it also made people question the definition of American democracy. Many people began to question how a democracy could keep half of its citizens—namely the female citizens—from voting and still consider themselves a beacon of equality. This, paired with admiration for women's contributions to the war effort, caused ever-growing support for suffrage. Though most women who had gone to work during the war to fill the roles vacated by men did return to their previous domestic lives, the belief that women were less important than men in society had been challenged.

Elizabeth Cady Stanton and Women's Rights

2

The Suffrage Movement

T he path to women's suffrage started as early as the 1800s. By the 1830s and 1840s, women had subtly begun to rebel against their societal exclusion from politics, labor, and self-reliance. Some, such as Margaret Fuller, held exclusively female "salons," or conversations, in their homes. The women who attended were asked to reflect upon their own experience of womanhood, and discussed gender-based limitations in their day-to-day lives. During these sessions, women began to challenge the notion that they were too frail or weak to be active participants in society. They questioned the notion that they lacked the intellect or fortitude of their male counterparts. In turn, they questioned the legitimacy of the ideals that kept them in their homes and away from being active participants in society. Women like Lucretia Mott, Elizabeth Cady Stanton, and Lucy

Opposite: This drawing shows Elizabeth Cady Stanton delivering her Declaration of Sentiments at the Seneca Falls Convention.

Stone also began to speak publicly about issues related to temperance, abolition, and religious restrictions. A change was in the making.

Wanting Change

One day over tea in the home of Jane Hunt in Waterloo, New York, Elizabeth Cady Stanton explained her frustration with the treatment of women that had long been weighing on her mind. Lucretia Coffin Mott, her sister Martha Coffin Wright, and Mary Ann M'Clintock were also there, and the five women decided that it was time to start fighting for change. There was growing demand for a convention solely devoted to women's rights, and out of this meeting, the Seneca Falls Convention was borne.

That afternoon, the women drew up an advertisement for a local paper, inviting those who believed in improving the conditions of womanhood to attend the two-day conference— exclusively women on the first day, with men welcomed on the second. They placed the ad in the *Seneca County Courier* with only eight days' notice. As news of the convention spread, other local newspapers also ran the advertisement.

The Seneca Falls Convention

On July 19 and 20, 1848, three hundred women and men gathered in Seneca Falls, New York, for the first women's rights convention in history. They had planned to hold it on such short notice so that it would align with Lucretia Mott's stay in town. Mott, who lived in Philadelphia, was one of very few women who achieved independent fame in this era. It was especially unusual that she was a celebrated orator, since women were often not allowed to speak in public.

The convention included several lectures, a humorous skit, and open discussions about organizing behind a single platform to fight for women's rights. Elizabeth Cady Stanton's famous **Declaration of Sentiments** was presented and voted on. Written in the style of the Declaration of Independence but directed toward the rights for women, it included female suffrage in its list of demands for women, even though many attendants thought the idea too extreme. There was great contention between those in favor of suffrage and those against it. However, from this debate, one very important person came forward to speak.

The only African American attendee, Frederick Douglass, the famous abolitionist, delivered a speech encouraging the people present to proceed with their fight by including suffrage. Even freed black men, he argued, had not yet been given the right to vote.

Despite these words, the list of resolutions was hotly debated. Eventually, and perhaps having been persuaded by Douglass, they reached a relative consensus, and it was put forth for signatures. Roughly one-third of those in attendance—sixty-eight women and thirty-two men—signed the document at the close of the convention. It included suffrage in its demands.

The Aftermath of Seneca Falls

The convention was highly sensationalized in the press, and several news sources covered it. While it gained national coverage, the reactions varied. Several newspapers came out in favor of women's rights, including suffrage, but many others claimed that if women were to become a part of the political world, the fabric of home life would fall apart.

This is widely held to be the beginning of the women's rights movement in the United States. In fact, in the book *History of Woman Suffrage*, Elizabeth Cady Stanton refers to this convention as the beginning of the movement.

The Seneca Falls Convention gave rise to many other similar events around the country, starting with the Rochester Women's Rights Convention in nearby Rochester, New York, only two weeks later. This event saw organizers elect a woman, Abigail Bush, to act as president of the convention. While the Seneca Falls Convention had followed previously established etiquette and elected a man to preside, the convention in Rochester would allow Abigail Bush to be the first woman in US history to preside over a public event with an integrated male and female audience.

In years to follow, more conventions cropped up around New York State, Ohio, Pennsylvania, and even as far away as Indiana. As support for local and regional conventions grew, organizers believed that a national convention—including the issues of women across all of the United States—was in order.

National Conventions

Following an abolitionist meeting in Boston, Massachusetts, on May 30, 1850, a large group of progressives, both male and female, met in Melodeon Hall to discuss planning a national convention. They envisioned an agenda and a list of speakers. Planners reached out to presenters, which included famous women's rights advocate and abolitionist poet Sojourner Truth and William Lloyd Garrison, the editor of the abolitionist newspaper *The Liberator*. Patricia Kellogg Wright Davis was chosen to serve as president of the Central Committee, the governing body responsible for planning and executing all such conventions. A date of October 23–24, 1850, at Brinley Hall in Worcester, Massachusetts, was chosen and advertisements made. The first National Women's Rights Convention had been staged.

The convention saw Brinley Hall filled beyond capacity, with many more people turned away at the door. Its incredible success encouraged eleven more conventions to follow.

Several propositions were put forth during the convention, including the idea that the word "male" be removed from the constitutions of each state, that women be allowed ownership of property, have access to education, and increased job opportunities outside the home.

LUCRETIA COFFIN MOTT

Born to a Quaker family in Nantucket, Massachusetts, in 1793, Lucretia Mott was raised believing in equality of all people, regardless of race or gender. She was highly educated, which was rare for women at this time, and became a teacher and Quaker minister. She grew interested in women's

An iconic image of Lucretia Mott

rights after noticing that male teachers were paid significantly more than she was, and through the Quakers, she became a prominent abolitionist.

Mott and her husband believed that slavery was a moral evil and worked to end it in the South through petitions, abolitionist involvement, and boycotting slave-produced goods like cane sugar and cotton. She was one of the founders of the Philadelphia Female Anti-Slavery Society, after she and several other women noticed that the other Anti-Slavery Societies often ignored the rights of slave women as a separate, important issue, and because many abolitionist groups did not agree with or allow women to actively participate in abolitionist events, still believing that women should be in the home.

Due to her oratory skill, Mott frequently traveled the United States, giving speeches at abolitionist events and later, women's conventions. It was unusual for women at this time to be public speakers, but her eloquence made her a desirable candidate for speaking engagements anyway.

While Mott initially thought the idea of fighting for women's suffrage was a mistake, because she feared it would make the women's rights movement look ridiculous, she later supported the idea and became one of its staunchest advocates. She served as the first president of the American Equal Rights Association, a universal suffrage group.

Mott was a **pacifist** and a leader of the Universal Peace Union, calling for an end to American involvement in wars. She also fought for women's rights on a local level, founding the Northern Association for the Relief and Employment of Poor Women in Philadelphia. She died in 1880, having lived a full life.

Key Early Suffragettes

Throughout the early decades of the women's movement, many women would play key roles and have a profound impact on future generations.

Elizabeth Cady Stanton and Susan B. Anthony forged a lifelong friendship that would inspire countless suffragettes.

Susan B. Anthony

Susan B. Anthony was born into a progressive Quaker family that believed in social equality. Her father and mother raised their seven children to be self-sufficient and manage their own affairs. Her father taught her math and business, despite the prevailing contemporary belief that women could or should not learn these things. Her parents also sent her to a boarding school to advance her education, but due to the Panic of 1837, they could no longer afford the tuition and she was forced, instead, to take a job teaching to help support her family.

She spent her early life committed to the cause of abolishing slavery, signing petitions to end forced labor as early as age seventeen. Her family was also active in abolitionsim, attending Universalist services that supported the cause, and hosting abolitionist meetings on their farm in Rochester, New York. Frederick Douglass was a regular visitor to their home and her lifelong friend.

Anthony spent her early life focused more on abolition than women's rights, and she would later say that initially she didn't care one way or another about voting. What she was passionate about was equal pay for equal work.

In 1851, she met Elizabeth Cady Stanton, who would be one of her closest friends and colleagues for the rest of her life. In fact, some biographers estimate that Stanton spent more time with Anthony than any other adult in her lifetime, including her family members, and even her husband. Their lifelong collaboration is one of the most memorable in the history of social reform, particularly in the fight for women's suffrage.

Elizabeth Cady Stanton

Elizabeth Cady was exposed to law early in life, spending time in her father's law library and debating legal issues with her father's law clerks. Her father, a one-term congressman and New York State supreme court judge, was often immersed in his work, while Stanton's mother, Margaret, suffered from severe depression. Because of this, Stanton spent a lot of time with her sister, Tryphena, and Tryphena's husband, Edward Bayard, who was also a lawyer. Stanton credits Bayard with showing her the ways in which laws privileged men over women. She was formally educated, which was unusual for the time, and attended the co-educational Johnstown Academy where she studied several languages, including Latin and Greek, mathematics, science, and literature. Upon completing her studies there, however, her choices of profession were limited. Because most colleges and universities did not accept women at that time, she attended a seminary school to continue her education.

She became involved in the abolitionist movement, and through her activities was introduced to Henry Brewster Stanton, a journalist, abolitionist orator, and lawyer. They were soon married. Throughout the marriage, she would call herself Elizabeth Cady Stanton, taking her husband's surname with her own, but refusing to be called "Mrs. Henry Brewster Stanton," as was custom of the time. She insisted that she was a separate person from her husband, deserving of her own name. Surprisingly, despite her fervent fight for women's suffrage, her husband did not believe in women's suffrage, which caused some discontent in the relationship.

When she and her husband moved to Boston, a hub of the abolitionist movement, Stanton became friends and intellectual allies with Louisa May Alcott, Frederick Douglass, Ralph Waldo Emerson, and many other important figures of the time. Through social discourse and political debate with these highly influential friends, her interest in abolition and civil rights grew.

When her husband grew ill, the family moved to Seneca Falls, New York, in hopes that it would improve Henry's health. Stanton was often lonely while living in this remote location after having spent much of her adult life surrounded by intellectual companionship in Boston. Her focus began to shift from the temperance and abolitionist movements to women's rights.

Lucy Stone

Lucy Stone was the first woman to graduate with a college degree in the state of Massachusetts in 1847, and was a gifted orator, gaining a following on the national circuit while she was still a very young woman. She was one of the main organizers of the national women's conventions, and presided over the seventh convention. She became the secretary of the Central Committee and acted in that capacity for nearly a decade. She was also a successful petitioner, delivering thousands of signatures in several campaigns for both the abolitionist and women's rights movements.

As a young teacher, she experienced gender and wage discrimination. It took great effort for her to achieve equal pay, but with the help of her students, she was eventually successful. These events shaped her opinions on women's issues, including suffrage.

She married Henry Blackwell in 1855, but kept her own last name, a highly unusual move for a woman during that time. Blackwell was a prominent abolitionist and a believer in women's suffrage. Stone and her husband would play prominent roles in the suffrage movement through their active participation in American Equal Rights Association (AERA), and later by founding the American Woman Suffrage Association (AWSA). When the National American Woman Suffrage Association (NAWSA) eventually formed, Stone was unanimously elected to chair the committee. Her speeches are credited as being some of the most influential in the women's movement, especially in recruiting new members.

Suffrage Organizations Take Hold

The women's rights movement had been steadily gaining momentum prior to the Civil War, and while it was somewhat less "important" during the years of the Civil War, it was not forgotten. Several important groups arose during this time, including the AERA, the NWSA,

AWSA, and the NAWSA. Of these only the NAWSA, a combination of the NSWA and the AWSA, survived into the twentieth century. It would become the most supported women's rights organization in the United States. The women who started it—Elizabeth Cady Stanton, Susan B. Anthony, and Lucy Stone—had great careers as champions of women's rights, which helped make the NAWSA such a success.

National American Woman Suffrage Association

The NAWSA began on February 18, 1890, having combined the NWSA and the AWSA. The newly formed NAWSA's mission was to push for all states to ratify a suffrage amendment to the US constitution. The group had seven thousand women at its inception, and by the early 1910s, that number had reached over two million, making it the largest voluntary organization in the country. Throughout its existence, the NAWSA would be the foremost group for women's suffrage in the United States; however, it was not without its faults. For instance, even as late as the 1900s, the organization refused to let women of color join. Members feared allowing women of color to join would dissuade some Southern supporters.

By 1910, largely because of the progressive movement and efforts initiated by the NAWSA, women's suffrage had begun to gain social and political approval. Membership in the NAWSA soared. In addition to this, a new young leader named Alice Paul emerged.

Alice Paul and the Woman Suffrage Procession

Alice Paul was a college-educated woman who became deeply involved with the suffrage movement while living in Britain. She gained notoriety for her visionary planning of suffrage events and her willingness to engage in **civil disobedience** in an attempt to gain equal legal status for women. When she returned to the United States, Paul ushered in a new era of suffrage protests. **Suffragettes** had previously pamphleted and petitioned for the right to vote, but Paul believed in using more radical means to bring about voting equality. Like the British suffragettes, Alice Paul believed that agitation was the most direct route to equality, and she staged protests and picketed the White House to bring awareness to suffrage.

She was one of the organizers of the Woman Suffrage Procession (sometimes called the Woman Suffrage Parade), which was staged on March 3, 1913, the day prior to Woodrow Wilson's presidential inauguration. It advanced much like any other parade. Famed suffragette and lawyer Inez Millholland led the group on horseback, wearing a crown and a long white cape. The procession was lively, with colorful floats and banners, women in yellow "suffragette" bunting, raucous music from multiple bands, squadrons of women marchers, and even horse-drawn chariots. They all marched under the banner "We Demand an Amendment to the United States Constitution Enfranchising the Women of the Country."

Despite Paul's attempts to procure more police presence on this day, there were not enough law enforcement officials on the scene. The half-million spectators pressed in so closely that often the women were forced to halt. Opposition from the crowd caused the whole thing to devolve into a riot, and the officers on duty refused to step in to stop the violence. People came forward to ridicule and physically beat the suffragettes.

After hearing about the event, a public dialogue around suffrage sprang up. The police brutality on that day gained the women sympathy and support, even from the people who had once opposed suffrage.

Women march in the Woman Suffrage Parade on March 3, 1913.

BRITISH SUFFRAGE

At the beginning of the twentieth century, women in Britain had their own suffrage movement, which would later inspire US suffragette Alice Paul. It was led by a woman named Emeline Pankhurst and her daughters, and gained a rapid following as the years progressed. Among Pankhurst's other accomplishments during this time was the founding of several organizations, including the Women's Social and Political Union (WSPU) in 1903. The WSPU would become the model used by suffrage groups worldwide.

British women often fought for voting rights by breaking windows, throwing rocks, and going on dangerously long **hunger strikes**. One British suffragette named Emily Davison even threw herself in front of the king on horseback, resulting in her death, becoming an immediate martyr for the cause. However, the suffragettes also experienced intense cruelty by those opposed to their movement, as well as law enforcement.

With the onset of World War I, Emeline Pankhurst called for a stop to suffrage activities, believing that the threat posed by Germany was a larger priority. However, the war became the movement's greatest boon. Women stepped into traditional male roles while men were away fighting in the war, and the effect women had on the war effort resulted in them being granted the right to vote in 1918.

Party Split

Paul brought a new kind of momentum with her, but it was not welcomed by all. Carrie Chapman Catt had successfully revived the suffrage movement as president of the NAWSA, and had a lot of success getting upper- and middle-class women on board with the movement. She believed that Paul's radical ideals would hurt the suffrage cause instead of help it. This presumption, along with Paul's tactics, caused the NAWSA to split. On one side was Paul's newly formed Congressional Union, later becoming the National Woman's Party (NWP) in 1916. On the other was Catt's NAWSA.

While the Congressional Union, and later the NWP, believed fervently in a national amendment to the constitution, thereby allowing all women the right to vote, the NAWSA sided on the state-by-state suffrage approach already in place. They put much of their energy into targeting states yet to pass suffrage. Between 1914 and 1917, they were a main driving force for state-by-state suffrage. And they had success. In those years, they spent much time targeting New York State, the most populated in the United States at that time, and one yet to grant suffrage to women living there. In 1917, the NAWSA's efforts were realized when suffrage passed in New York, marking a major victory for suffragettes.

As early as 1916, however, the NAWSA's tactics were wearing thin. It was becoming clear that many Southern states would not grant voting rights to women without a passed federal amendment. Catt called for an emergency convention, during which she introduced her "Winning Plan." This plan shifted focus from state-by-state suffrage to a more universal suffrage and the push for a federal amendment. The organization would use professional lobbyists to pressure both the Republican and Democratic parties to support suffrage.

The Saga of the Anthony Amendment

The "Susan B. Anthony amendment" was initially introduced to Congress by Aaron A. Sargent of California in 1878. It was written exactly like the Fifteenth Amendment, which called for an end to voter prohibition based on that person's "race, color, or previous condition of servitude," except it focused on sex instead of race. Sargent was a supporter of suffrage and a friend of Susan B. Anthony, and he had unsuccessfully tried to slip suffrage provisions into unrelated bills several times prior to the introduction of this amendment. Despite limited support for the bill, it did not go to the floor for a vote until 1887, when it was easily defeated.

It wasn't until 1914 that it was again put forth for a vote. By this time, the NAWSA had several successes nationwide, particularly in Western states where women were granted suffrage. Despite this momentum, the bill failed again, but this time by a smaller margin. This setback caused the NAWSA to focus their energy on other big states yet to pass suffrage.

In 1917, the country went to war, upsetting family lives and introducing many new opportunities for people to voice opinions. Carrie Chapman Catt took advantage of this opportunity and refocused the NAWSA on aiding the war effort. While Alice Paul disagreed with this move, claiming that supporting the war effort took time and resources away from the fight for suffrage, which was the NWP's sole aim, Catt succeeded in gaining public support for the cause by showing the NAWSA as a patriotic organization. Three NAWSA members were appointed to the Women's Committee for the Council of National Defense, which

Carrie Chapman Catt made major strides toward suffrage as president of the NAWSA.

allocated resources and increased morale during wartime. This encouraged favor among the American public for the suffrage cause.

As a direct result of the NAWSA's efforts and a shift in public sentiment following the war, there was another push for a federal amendment to be considered. The House again voted on the Anthony amendment, and this time it passed. However, the final decision sat with the Senate. In 1918, it was defeated there by two votes. Dissatisfied yet determined, the NAWSA undertook campaigns to unseat senators opposed to suffrage in several elections, successfully unseating two of those opposed.

Opposition

While today it may seem ridiculous to oppose a woman's right to vote, there was strong opposition to voting rights for much of the suffragette movement.

Ironically, some of the staunchest anti-suffrage supporters were women themselves. Many women saw suffrage—and even the entire women's rights movement—as a threat to the structure and flow of family life. They worried that women would lose their valued position in the home, and that the sacred role of caretaker might slip away if they were given the same rights as men.

The opposition began informally, but eventually, anti-suffragists organized into formal groups to oppose women voting. In 1911, the National Association Opposed to

THE SILENT SENTINELS AND THE NIGHT OF TERROR

The Silent Sentinels, so called for their silent protests, were groups of women who sat in front of the White House six days a week, beginning on January 10, 1917. They picketed each day, peacefully holding signs with pro-suffrage slogans until June 4, 1919, when the national amendment passed in the House and the Senate. While these women were practicing civil disobedience, they were frequently attacked, often by male passersby who disagreed with their message. They were sometimes arrested under lesser charges like obstructing traffic. These women, when arrested, often spent time in the Occoquan Workhouse, where conditions were so unsanitary that bugs and worms were frequently found in their food.

On November 14, 1917, the superintendent of the Occoquan Workhouse decided to take matters into his own hands and teach the suffragettes a lesson. This night would come to be known as the **Night of Terror**. Forty guards were ordered to brutalize the women. The women were dragged from their beds in the middle of the night, beaten and kicked, chained with their arms above their heads for the night, or worse. Of the thirty-three suffragists held in the prison, not one of them escaped torture that night.

This created bad press for President Woodrow Wilson, and the nation began to move toward the side of suffragists. Later, the Supreme Court ruled that these women had all been illegally arrested, illegally convicted, and illegally jailed.

Woman Suffrage (NAOWS) was founded to fight against suffrage nationally. They had more than 350,000 members, and while the organization was largely male, it was run by Josephine Dodge, a woman. The NAOWS opposed the vote on the grounds that if women were to become involved in politics, they would not remain impartial enough to further the women's rights movement in more practical ways. Between 1912 and 1916, the group grew in numbers and momentum, successfully blocking more than thirty suffrage referenda.

The Nineteenth Amendment

By the end of World War I, with public support largely in favor of suffrage, an amendment to the constitution reached the floor of the Senate once again. This time, it passed in both houses and went to the states for ratification.

The NAWSA had previously organized ratification committees in each state, and fearing public sentiment would turn against suffrage as the memory of women's roles during the war faded, resources were immediately diverted to these committees who would, in turn, put pressure on state legislators to ratify.

In the end, they were successful. After seven decades of actively fighting for suffrage, the Nineteenth Amendment was passed on August 18, 1920, guaranteeing all women the right to vote.

WHEN DID WOMEN BEGIN TO VOTE?

1881 Isle of Man

1893 New Zealand

1902 Australia (Except
    Aboriginal Women)

1906 Finland

1913 Norway

1915 Iceland

1917 Canadian women who had
    male relatives serving in
    the war

1918 Canada (Except
    First Nations)

1918 Germany

1919 Belgium gives war widows
    and mothers of fallen
    soldiers the right to vote, as
    well as women held by the
    enemy as political prisoners
    during the war.

1920 United States

1921 Sweden

1924 Saint Lucia

1928 Britain and Ireland

1929 Ecuador

1931 Spain

1934 Turkey

1944 France

1945 Italy

1947 Mexico

1948 Belgium

1949 China

1950 India

1950 Canadian First Nations
    (Quebec in 1969)

1954 Colombia

1957 Malaysia

1962 Aboriginal People
    in Australia

1963 Iran

1964 Libya

1965 Afghanistan (Revoked under
    Taliban, 1996–2001)

1967 Ecuador

1971 Switzerland

1972 Bangladesh

1976 Portugal

1994 South Africa

2002 Bahrain

2006 United Arab Emirates

2011 Saudi Arabia

Women Fight for Equality Through Other Means

W omen like Susan B. Anthony and Alice Paul fought hard for suffrage by using legal means, but there were many other suffragettes who brought women's rights and equality to the forefront of the American public using other methods. Women were becoming involved in areas previously considered to be exclusively masculine: art, music, health, and more.

These women made impacts in other, unforgettable ways. Many contributed to American support for, and discussion of, suffrage and women's issues. The suffragettes led the way by championing equality with the vote, but other women brought awareness to the cause, and forged ahead in new areas.

Opposite: *Hull House, the first of many settlement houses in the United States*

Settlement Houses

Jane Addams was arguably one of the most influential women of her time. She was an author, activist, pacifist, suffragette, and co-founder of the first **settlement houses** in the United States.

Started in Chicago, Illinois, Hull House, so named for Charles Hull, who had once owned the mansion Addams and her colleague Ellen Gates Starr rented, became a meeting place and community center that would thrive for more than one hundred years. By 1911, Hull House had expanded to thirteen buildings. Addams and Starr ran a preschool for children of immigrants, a boys' club to give teens a way to stay out of trouble, and night school for adults. They offered discussions, art exhibits, readings, and lectures on a variety of social topics. They opened the first playground in Chicago, and grew to provide a house for single, working women to live in, and a coffee shop to provide a space for adults to get together socially. They collected data on illness and poverty, fought for sanitation and a juvenile court system, and campaigned against sweatshops.

Due to Addams and Starr's efforts, settlement houses became successful and effective, appearing in other areas around the United States. By 1920 there were almost five hundred serving impoverished urban areas. These houses provided the first social welfare to struggling families in the country and created a framework for programs like the **New Deal** after World War II.

African Americans Who Fought for Women's Rights

Despite growing out of the abolitionist movement, the women's movement was often exclusionary to women of color. However, there were several African Americans who fought for women's rights in the early twentieth century.

One of the staunchest supporters of African American women's suffrage was W. E. B. Du Bois, the famed civil rights activist. He regularly contributed to the cause of suffrage by writing about the importance of African American women gaining the vote. As the editor of *The Crisis*, the official magazine for the National Association for the Advancement of Colored People (NAACP), he regularly ran columns and commentary with a pro-suffrage message. He even published special editions of the magazine devoted wholly to suffrage. One of these special editions was published just before the New York State referendum for suffrage in 1917, and may have helped sway the public toward giving women that right.

Daisy Elizabeth Adams Lampkin held suffragette meetings in her home in suburban Pennsylvania, gathering women together to focus on issues that particularly affected their lives as African American housewives. When she and her husband moved into the city of Pittsburgh, she became active with local suffrage groups. She joined the Lucy Stone League (formerly known as the New Negro Women's Equal Franchise Federation), and by 1915 she was elected

Ida B. Wells, circa 1893

to president of the organization, a post she held for forty years. She organized African American women into consumer groups and gave impromptu speeches on busy street corners about the importance of suffrage, among other women's rights issues.

Ida B. Wells, in addition to being an African American rights activist throughout the Progressive Era, opened her own suffrage organization called Alpha Suffrage Club. Even after Alice Paul announced that there would be no African American women in the 1913 Woman Suffrage Parade, Wells and forty women from her chapter arrived and demanded to march. When Alice Paul reluctantly allowed them space in the back, Wells broke rank and walked alongside her white friends in the procession.

The New Woman

There was a new kind of woman emerging in society in the 1900s, one who was independent, well educated, a feminist, and progressive. Aptly called the **New Woman**, these women often graduated from college with degrees in their field of choice. They valued autonomy and made their own decisions. The New Woman was often the subject of period artwork and literature, including Charles Dana Gibson's *The Reason Dinner was Late* and the popular plays of Henrik Ibsen, such as *A Doll's House*.

While the New Woman was a popular icon in American society, what made a woman one was often disputed. For some, it was involvement in politics or sporting events previously denied women. For others, it was having career options beyond teaching or nursing. And for others still it was simply a fashion statement that broke from the old way of dressing. As time went on, variations on the New Woman would arise, from giddy **flapper** to headstrong feminist, but they all had one thing in common: they were the changing face of American womanhood.

Art and Female Artists

While women were heavily involved in all aspects of the professional art world by the 1920s, one arena they struggled to gain a foothold in throughout the early nineteenth century was visual art. Most of the art that women made prior to this time was considered domestic art, more on the level of crafts, and included art forms such as weaving and textile production, pottery, and tapestry. Women who pursued arts like sculpting and painting were often banned from attending art schools or dismissed by male artists, who they might have apprenticed. In fact, most women who succeeded in gaining a formal education in visual art prior to the late 1800s came from families of artists, and were instructed by their parents or other family members. This meant that many women who learned visual art were self-taught, which made gaining recognition in the art world even harder. While a handful of female artists gained prestige in the eighteenth and nineteenth centuries, including British artists Mary Moser and Angelica

SUFFRAGETTE CARTOONISTS

Some of the most visual outcries for suffrage came from talented women who fought using political cartoons. Cartoonism was a field that few women had entered prior to the twentieth century. In reply to political cartoons condemning suffrage, female artists like Nina Allender, the National Woman's Party cartoonist, and Ida Proper Sedgewick, the art editor for *Woman Voter*, used their artwork to fight back and gain support for their cause, pushing the suffrage movement forward. They often depicted working-women or "the New Woman" of the 1900s to forge a bond with working-class women. They turned the tables on the anti-suffrage cartoons drawn by men by using the men's media against them.

This political cartoon, drawn in 1915, shows Lady Liberty carrying the torch for women's suffrage to the Eastern states.

Kauffman, it wasn't until the twentieth century that new opportunities for female artists arrived.

At the turn of the twentieth century, art became a more acceptable profession for women, and art schools began to accept and confer degrees to women. There were obstacles even then, however. For example, many thought women were too modest to look upon a nude model to learn to draw the human body. Likewise, women were initially ineligible for art prizes and individual art shows. From the late 1800s on, however, there was an influx of notable female artists. Marguerite Zorach, Alice Neel, Jennie Augusta Brownscombe, and Georgia O'Keeffe all made strides for women in art by attending art colleges, winning awards typically only conferred to men, and having independent shows of their work.

Fashion

Prior to the 1850s, when the first wave of suffrage swept the United States, women's dresses were quite elaborate. They often involved corsets that hugged the body so tightly as to cause physical pain and injury, giant skirts that billowed out and weighed the wearer down, and sweeping trains that could easily get caught on uneven floors or underneath the sole of an unsuspecting shoe. In fact, women's clothing was so large and heavy that moving about was considered quite an ordeal and often limited women in their daily activities. Many physicians pointed out the health dangers these fashions posed, but women largely ignored their advice.

By 1900, women's fashion had grown to include large, gaudy hats that often featured decorative flowers, intricate ribbons, and sometimes even dead, stuffed birds. These hats, due to their weight and intricacy, often needed hatpins to hold them in place. Each pin stuck into the side of the hat, securing it to a woman's hair. Some could be up to 12 inches (30 centimeters) in length! Surprisingly, these pins would serve a new purpose in the quest for women's rights. As women began to venture out more often without chaperones, men tried to take advantage of them. "Mashers," as the lecherous men were called, would often use pet names to speak to women, or even touch a woman without her permission. Women exercised their independence, and demonstrated their ability to protect themselves, by using hatpins as weapons to stab or prick a masher who was giving them grief.

By the 1920s, fashion trends saw the biggest change yet. Perhaps somewhat inspired by the freedoms suffragettes had fought so hard to obtain for women a few years earlier, some began assuming more free forms of dress. Called flappers, they wore their skirts short—which at this time meant calf-length—and their hair bobbed. These trends were considered both scandalous and intriguing, yet met with outrage from much of the American public.

Others prospered off the shift in fashion. Coco Chanel, for instance, made a name for herself not just as a perfumer and fashion icon but also as a designer during this era. Creating sailor suits for women, little black dresses for any occasion, and using jersey and crepe fabrics, she glamorized the drop-waisted frock and changed the way women primarily in Europe and the United States dressed forever.

Along with this new dress code, new behaviors arose that many people assumed to be linked to the fashion craze. For example, women began smoking and dancing in public, openly engaging in hand holding or kissing with partners before marriage, and speakeasies allowed them an opportunity to drink socially with men, where formerly the only women in saloons were prostitutes and "loose women."

Music and Film

Whether it was singing lullabies to their children or singing battle cries in protest, music has always been important to the history of women. Before television and radio, music and singalongs were the major form of entertainment for families and communities. Choir was important for church, and many women participated in church choir as one of the few creative outlets allowed to them. Slaves had long used music to provide a rhythm to the work they did or to communicate information in code to one another.

Music was used as a way to promote suffrage from early in the movement. They created hymns and battle marches that included songs like, "Shall Women Vote?" and, "Oh, Dear, What Can the Matter Be?" In Britain, Ethyl Smith composed, "March of the Women," which later became the anthem of the British suffragette movement.

African American women also used music to fight inequality. In 1933, Florence Price became the first African American woman to have a piece performed by a major orchestra in the United States. Interestingly, the woman who performed it, Margaret Bonds, was the first African American to perform as a soloist in the Chicago Symphony Orchestra.

Jazz music created a new opportunity for liberation by providing new job opportunities for women and creating a social scene where women were welcome. Prior to jazz, most popular music was performed by primarily white male musicians, but Ma Rainey, Bessie Smith, Lil' Hardin, Billie Holiday, and Ella Fitzgerald became popular performers of the day, inspiring women around the country with their beautiful voices and new melodies. Jazz music inspired a series of Broadway musicals starting in the late 1920s, which provided women new opportunities on stage.

Jazz music also encouraged an overlap between arts and genres for women. Gertrude Abercrombie, a prominent jazz artist from Chicago, held jam sessions and jazz parties at her house, and used jazz music as an inspiration for her artwork.

Advertising began to change during the jazz era, too. Flappers and the "New Woman" created a new customer base with disposable income. As young, single women went to work and used that money to buy their own things, an increasing amount of advertising was directed at them. In addition to groceries and cleaning products, which had always been marketed to women, now luxury items—clothing, cigarettes, and even cars—were being marketed to them as well. These

This 1920s illustration depicts the stereotypical New Woman: fashion-forward and independent women.

ads capitalized on the image of the New Woman by making claims like, "The new woman is using our product!"

As women began to perform with increasing frequency on stage and then in film, the rise of the female celebrity began. Torn between a world where she was largely objectified and being able to earn her own income using performance, the female celebrity provided new sources of inspiration to women. Actresses like Louise Brooks drove flapper fashion trends and showed America what the New Woman was like. Soon actresses like Greta Garbo, Anna May Wong, and Delores Del Rio rose to fame, paving the way for female actresses to be taken seriously as performers and widely admired in society.

Literature

Despite some gender barriers, women have always been more welcome in the world of writing than in other ventures. From Christine de Pisan in the 1400s to Jane Austen in 1800s, right up to Alice Walker in the 1970s, women have been creating strong female characters in literature almost as long as literature has existed.

During the abolitionist movement of the 1800s, the suffrage movement of the 1900s, and the jazz era of the 1920s, women often used literature as a way to offer a view from another perspective. Some writers chose nonfiction to make their voices heard, while others illustrated through fiction or poetry. Indeed, many women would publish works as contributors, editors, or anonymously throughout the nineteenth and twentieth centuries. One of the most powerful pieces of literature during the abolitionist movement was Harriet Beecher Stowe's *Uncle Tom's Cabin*, which showed the plight of African American men and women living on plantations in the South. Stowe's novel is often credited as helping start the Civil War. In the mid-1800s, author and editor Julia Ward Howe wrote about dissatisfaction with women's roles, particularly that of "wife," in her novels and poetry. Drawing from her own experiences, she examined the plight of women stuck in marriages where they were beholden to a man they no longer loved or trusted. In the 1900s, Gertrude Stein used writing to bring attention to women living alternative lifestyles. Her work *Tender Buttons*, published in 1912, is often exalted by modern feminists for her use of language to convey an "otherness" in feminine objects, and her veiled descriptions of ordinary objects representative of a women's mind and body.

Female authors often played the role of activist in other ways. Edith Wharton, the first woman to be awarded the Pulitzer Prize for fiction, was an American living in Paris during World War I. She was already quite wealthy and famous by that time, enjoying an autonomy known to few women of the era, but instead of returning to the United States, she stayed to aid the people of France and the refugees of war-torn Belgium. She started schools and hospitals, workrooms for seamstresses, and even opened her own home as a place of rest to women refugees.

In the decades that followed, literature—both fiction and nonfiction—would continue to play an important role in women's liberation.

Sports

Women's inclusion in athletics began with the most American sport around, baseball. In 1866, Vassar College had two female baseball teams, organized by the girls themselves in

Women achieved new levels of independence thanks to the invention of the bicycle.

defiance to other "sports" offered to them by the college, which included gardening. They played in long skirts, as there was no fashion alternative for athletics for women at that time. Despite the limited mobility, baseball caught on among women, and in 1890, the Bloomers, an all-female baseball team, began touring the country and competing against men's teams. By the 1930s, other professional women baseball teams would emerge, like the All-American Redheads.

By 1896, the first female intercollegiate basketball games were being organized. The first match between Stanford and the University of California at Berkley scandalized the nation. Not only was it uncommon for women to perform in front of an audience, but an athletic match was particularly unusual. Regardless, spectators watched—even young men, who had been prohibited from attending due to concerns over modesty but had snuck in to the match anyway.

In 1900, women were included for the first time in the Olympic games, which were held in Paris that year. The only events for women that first year were lawn tennis and golf, but in 1912 they added women's swimming (the United States did not compete because of modesty concerns), and in 1928 women's track and field.

BICYCLES

One unexpected development that aided women in gaining independence was the bicycle. A bicycle was easy to use, fun to ride, and useful for improving health through exercise—all with the added benefit of providing wider mobility to women to travel, visit, and complete their own errands. Susan B. Anthony was quoted in *New York World*'s as saying that bicycling had "done more to emancipate women than anything else in the world."

In the 1870s, the "safety" bicycle was developed for women and the elderly. Instead of changing the size of the front tire to determine speed, these bicycles introduced the use of a chain to allow the pedals to distribute power evenly between both wheels. This allowed more women than ever to use the bicycle as a means of transportation.

Beyond providing women with affordable and practical transportation, bicycles came to symbolize something more for the women's movement. They taught women self-reliance and gave them courage to try new things and go into new situations. They became both literally and metaphorically a symbol of freedom and adventure for women.

VOTES FOR WOMEN A SUCCESS

NORTH AMERICA PROVES IT

White—Full Suffrage
Dotted—Presidential Suffrage
Crosses—Primary Suffrage
Black—No Suffrage

The Canadian provinces of British Columbia, Alberta, Saskatchewan and Manitoba extended full suffrage to their women in 1916. Ontario gave them full suffrage in March, 1917.

**How long will the Republic of the United States
lag behind the Monarchy of Canada?**

NATIONAL WOMAN SUFFRAGE PUBLISHING COMPANY, Inc.

171 Madison Avenue   154   **New York City**

August, 1917

The Nineteenth Amendment and What Came Next

By 1917, various women's organizations were stepping up their momentum and advocating for the creation of a federal amendment for women's suffrage. The NAWSA had spent much of its existence pushing individual states to decide whether women living there could vote or not. In many instances, they had been successful. Several Western states had granted women full suffrage, including Washington, Nevada, and California. Some Eastern states, like New York and Michigan, had too. Several states had also given voting rights to women in regard to the school board, as schooling and children were believed to be in a woman's domain. In some states, women could even vote in presidential elections. However, problems continued to arise with states that did not allow women to vote at all. It became apparent

Opposite: This map shows the state of women's suffrage in North America circa 1917.

that a federal amendment was needed to realize the dream of countrywide suffrage.

Leading to the Nineteenth Amendment

Once again, women's organizations put pressure on Congress. In 1918, mid-term elections were held, and several seats in the House and Senate would be voted upon. The National Woman's Party organized women in the states that granted full suffrage to promote whichever House and Senate candidates supported women gaining the right to vote. They believed that by stacking the vote in favor of suffrage in the House and Senate, they could pass a federal amendment. They campaigned for the candidates who were pro-suffrage by targeting the races where they would be most likely to win. They canvassed, put up billboards, and staged speaking tours encouraging people to get to the **ballot** and voice their dissatisfaction with the status quo. Their cross-country motorcades and publicity stunts also helped many pro-suffrage candidates win.

Woodrow Wilson had opposed suffrage in his first term as president. Despite his own daughter's involvement with the suffrage movement, he initially believed that suffrage was best left to state legislators to decide. However, now in his second term, he had received a lot of negative attention, especially for the treatment of the suffragettes kept in the Occoquan Workhouse. Reports of the physical abuse shocked him, and he was moved to action. Starting in

1918, he altered his stance and publicly supported a federal amendment calling for women's suffrage, citing the women's effort during World War I as the reason he changed his mind. Wilson addressed the Senate that same year, a very unusual occurrence for a commander in chief, urging them to vote in favor of suffrage. During his speech, he famously asked the gathered officials, "We have made partners of the women in this war ... Shall we admit them only to a partnership of suffering and sacrifice and toil and not to a partnership of privilege and right?" Despite his urging, the vote failed by two votes.

A year later, on May 21, 1919, James R. Mann, Republican Congressman from Illinois, proposed the Nineteenth Amendment, calling for female suffrage. It became affectionately known as the "Susan B. Anthony amendment" and easily passed in the House, but when it got to the Senate for ratification, it came down to two votes. Now, three-fourths of the states had to ratify the amendment for it to become law. In Tennessee, the last state to ratify and make the three-fourths majority, it actually came down to one vote. Harry T. Burn, only twenty-three years old, was undecided. However, he then received word from his mother, urging him to vote for suffrage. While he personally did not support suffrage, he thought that he ought to listen to his mother. His vote helped make history.

On August 26, 1920, then Secretary of State Bainbridge Colby certified the amendment. In November, millions of women voted in elections for the first time.

Alice Paul celebrates the passage of the Nineteenth Amendment from her balcony.

Late Ratification

Thirty-six of the forty-eight states ratified the Nineteenth Amendment by 1920, though twelve states refused to ratify on principle. Women in these states could vote, but these twelve states would not ratify because of their disapproval of such a law. Ratification after 1920 was purely ceremonial, though it certainly sent a message to women that they were still not considered equal. Connecticut ratified only a month after the amendment was passed, followed by Vermont in 1921 and Delaware in 1923. Maryland ratified in 1941, though they did not certify the ratification until 1958.

The National Woman's Party, led by Alice Paul, however, saw that having the right to vote was not enough to make women equal. The NWP continued to fight for women's rights by promoting an additional amendment to the Constitution, called the Equal Rights Amendment, or the "Lucretia Mott amendment." Penned by Alice Paul, the amendment held that women would have equal rights with men and be equal citizens. It was first introduced to Congress in 1923, and reintroduced annually for decades, but only made it to the floor for a vote once. This was in 1946, when it was defeated by three votes in the Senate. While men feared the amendment because they were highly privileged by the law, working-class women also disliked the amendment because they worried it would take away the "protection of women" that existed in the 1920s. This included things like constraints on female labor and working-hour limits. Others worried that an equal rights amendment would take away some benefits women held in society, such as being immune to **conscription** and being financially supported by their husbands.

While Alice Paul and other feminist activists fought for the amendment, the arguments against it played on some of the worst fears of Americans. For instance, if men and women were given equal access to all education, it would mean that all schools would have to be co-educational, a prospect that did not sit well with many Americans.

Perhaps the most famous name among those opposed to the Equal Rights Amendment was Phyllis Schlafly, a conservative family values activist and lawyer from St. Louis, Missouri. Schlafly organized the STOP (an acronym for Stop Taking Our Privileges) Equal Rights Amendment campaign, which ran for all the years that the Equal Rights Amendment was up for ratification at the state level. She articulately argued that making women legally equal would break down the family unit, leave widows without their husband's social security benefits, and send women into war. She also believed that it would end alimony and child support settlements that usually benefitted women in cases of divorce. Through her anti-feminist organization Eagle Forum, she and her followers focused on restoring family values to the United States and fighting against what they considered threats to the traditional family unit.

The amendment did not pass a vote on the House and Senate floors until 1972, nearly fifty years after Alice Paul introduced it. However, even though it passed in the House and Senate, it still had to be ratified by three-fourths of the states to become law. Thirty-five states of the needed thirty-eight ratified, but five of those states rescinded their ratification before the deadline in 1979. Even after being granted a three-year extension, not enough states ratified for it to become law. In 1983, the law was reintroduced to the House of Representatives but failed to get enough votes to be heard in Congress.

Despite this, the Equal Rights Amendment is still proposed each year in Congress, and several people have been instrumental in gaining support for it, among them

Senators Tammy Baldwin and Ted Kennedy. In 2011, Tammy Baldwin, a United States senator from Wisconsin, moved that the former deadline be removed from the bill. From 1983 until his death in 2009, Democratic Senator from Massachusetts Ted Kennedy championed the bill, and was later joined by Democratic Senators Bob Menendez from New Jersey and Carol Maloney from New York. While it has been reintroduced with updated text as recently as 2013, it has not yet passed a vote to be reintroduced for ratification.

Twenty-four states have statewide versions of the Equal Rights Amendment as of 2016. Most of these states, like Colorado, Wyoming, and Utah, are Western states that have traditionally allowed more equality for women than Northeastern or Southern states. The language differs from state to state, but none put it so eloquently as Wyoming in their state constitution: "In their inherent right to life, liberty and the pursuit of happiness, all members of the human race are equal."

The Impact of the Great Depression on Women

While the 1920s were a time of prosperity in the United States, the stock market crash of 1929 and the subsequent depression caused new hardships for families. The unemployment rate had been about 3 percent before the crash, but by 1933, it was up to 25 percent. Banks closed, and families could not withdraw their money. People could no longer afford anything beyond the most essential items, which caused stores to close their doors. This in turn increased unemployment. Some people when faced with the sudden prospect of being destitute even committed suicide.

Poverty was at an all-time high, and many families became homeless, looking for work in other parts of the country. Many lived in makeshift tents and lean-tos in fields or vacant lots. Families were often without food for long periods of time. Many stood in ration lines to buy small amounts of food available, waited for charity workers to bring loaves of bread, begged, or scavenged to find food.

The Great Depression forced many families into poverty.

This affected women in different ways from men. Women who had taken jobs prior to the crash often lost them, since factories and shops where women often worked shut down. Women were tasked with feeding their families on very little, which entailed finding food, making meals and clothing from the cheapest materials available and then making them last, or trying to bring money in by begging, selling apples or other goods on street corners, or waiting in charity lines. It was a bad situation for poor white women in the North, but it was even worse for African American women in the South. The unemployment rate for African Americans soared to 50 percent as the jobs that they once occupied were offered to white men first. African American women were already paid only a fraction of what white women were paid, and those women only a fraction of what white men made. This meant African American women were often doing grueling work for almost no pay.

Eleanor Roosevelt

Franklin Roosevelt's New Deal economic plan was designed to spurn growth in the economy by implementing a "bottom-up" approach that began by employing people in public works projects. While many economists credit him with pulling the nation out of the depression, it was his wife, Eleanor, who made a difference for women. Eleanor, who never openly supported suffrage but joined the League of Women Voters in 1920, was a strong advocate for women's rights, often influencing her husband to think of women in a new light.

Franklin Roosevelt chose women to head new government agencies, like Frances Perkins, who helped develop the Social Security Plan, and Mary McLeod Bethune, the first African American to head a government agency in the United States.

Eleanor Roosevelt fought vehemently for women to be actively involved in politics, joining and supporting a variety of women's rights organizations and publishing several articles and books about the importance of women's voices in politics. As the country prepared for World War II, she advocated for female involvement in the military and championed women taking jobs to help the war effort at home in munitions factories.

Even after her husband's death, she remained active in politics and women's rights. She pressured John F. Kennedy to create the first Presidential Commission on the Status of Women, and served as its chair. Despite her opposition to the Equal Rights Amendment, many consider Eleanor Roosevelt to be one of the best feminist role models in this nation's history.

Women in Another Great War

After the Japanese bombing of Pearl Harbor on December 7, 1941, the United States was forced into another World War. As with the previous conflict, many jobs occupied by men were left to women as men fought overseas. This war was different for women, though. Not only was the First Lady championing women going to work, but women were being

MARY MCLEOD BETHUNE

One of the most important African Americans in United States history, Mary McLeod Bethune was often called "the First Lady of the Struggle." Born to former slaves in 1875, she was one of seventeen children, and grew up in rural South Carolina during segregation. She became an educator first, founding the Daytona Educational and Industrial School for Negro Girls in 1904. She fought for African American rights at a time when there were few, and for women's rights on a local, state, and federal level. She served as an officer in the National Association of Colored Women before founding and presiding over her own organization, the National Council of Negro Women. This group focused on creating opportunities for African American women and ending segregation. She was active in the NAACP and the National Urban League.

In 1936, she was appointed by President Roosevelt director of Negro Affairs for the National Youth Administration. While her attempts to pass legislation to help African Americans were often shot down, she brought issues like equal pay and lynching to the public eye. She also served as special assistant to the secretary of war during World War II, and the director of the Women's Army Corps, where she pushed for African American women to be able to join the military.

The first women to serve in the United States military were still expected to wear "feminine" dress such as skirts and high heels.

deployed in record numbers. In addition to nearly eighty thousand women who went as nurses, three hundred fifty thousand women went as soldiers, something that had never before happened with government sanction in US history.

Women were mostly sent as secretaries, file clerks, and radio operators—traditionally more "feminine" roles—but they were also code breakers, electricians, and medics. Agnes Meyer Driscoll, for instance, worked as a cryptanalyst for the code and signal department of the navy during World War I and World War II, and helped develop the cypher machine used by the navy through the 1920s. In 1943, Dr. Margaret

Craighill became the first doctor in the United States Army Medical Corps, after years of women only being allowed as nurses. These women broke through barriers that had kept women from these jobs prior to wartime by doing exemplary work in new fields.

One of the biggest advancements for women during this time was the ability for them to serve as soldiers. Women generally served in all-female battalions under female directors in the Women's Army Corps (WAC), Women Accepted for Volunteer Emergency Service (WAVES) in the naval forces, United States Coast Guard Women's Reserve (SPARS), or the Women Air Force Service Pilots (WASPs). These groups were often exclusionary to women of color, however. In fact, the WASPs did not allow any African American women at all, though they had a few Chinese American, Mexican American, and Native American women in their ranks. While these organizations were recognized as reserve units and not active military groups, the Women's Armed Services Integration Act of 1948, which allowed women to serve as permanent, active military members, was a direct result of their involvement.

The WASPs especially added a new dimension to the role of women in the armed forces by employing women as pilots. This allowed men to fight in direct combat, which the women were not trained to do. Despite their war efforts, they have been largely forgotten by history. In 1944, when faced with the choice to either fully incorporate the women into the military, allowing them to receive veteran benefits and full military honors, or disband them, the choice was made to disband. The women who served did not receive the World War II Victory Medal until 1984.

Changing Mindsets

During World War II, many US sports teams were forced to close because they didn't have enough players. Chewing gum mogul and Chicago White Sox owner Philip K. Wrigley, however, worried about what closing would do to the future of baseball. He decided to start an all-female league to keep interest and profits going through the war. The All-American Girls Softball League was formed in 1943.

The women on the teams never played regulation baseball, but something in between baseball and softball. Despite some initial criticism, the league grew very popular, with hundreds of thousands of spectators frequenting games. The women were paid salaries much smaller than what the professional men in Major League Baseball were paid, and they were forced to play in skirts, but it brought female athletics to a larger scale than ever. The league was disbanded in 1954 after at least six hundred women had competed in a professional sport.

Upon returning from World War II, men were granted their old jobs and women were expected to go back to their former, mainly domestic ways of life. But many women did not want that. They had experienced new opportunities, learned new trades, and became valuable contributors to society. For many, having these experiences propelled them into a renewed interest in fighting for women's rights.

ROSIE THE RIVETER

Rosie the Riveter became a feminist icon during World War II, and is still commonly used by feminist groups today.

One of the most iconic images from World War II is one known as "Rosie the Riveter." The poster, which depicts a feminine white woman in factory clothes and a bandana pulling up her sleeve to reveal a strong bicep, bears the phrase, "We can do it!" J. Howard Millner's illustration was created as part of a series of posters supporting the war effort. Westinghouse had commissioned the posters as part of a propaganda campaign encouraging women to work in munitions factories and taking over traditionally male responsibilities to help out. The *Saturday Evening Post* would later feature on its cover a version of Rosie depicted by esteemed artist Norman Rockwell, and various government propaganda ads would run pictures of real-life Rosies—women photographed in similar poses who were stepping up to do their part began appearing in advertising across the country. Today, this icon is still commonly seen and reimagined.

How Suffragettes Changed the World

While gender equality still has not been achieved in all areas in American life, women have made giant leaps forward from the time of the suffragettes. The legacy of those who fought to give women the vote has inspired countless other women to push for equal rights in the United States and beyond.

Waves of Feminism

Throughout the nineteenth, twentieth, and twenty-first centuries, there have been three eras, or waves, of feminism. Each wave targeted different struggles facing women and others during that time. The **first-wave feminists**—the suffragettes—focused on big issues like voting rights and property ownership. The second wave, taking place in the

Opposite: *Second-wave feminists march to protest inequality in August 1970.*

1960s, 1970s, and 1980s, included issues like sexuality, family roles, and pay inequality. Called the Women's Liberation Movement, feminists fought against the patriarchy with renewed vigor. The third wave of feminism, starting in the 1990s and continuing today, champions inclusion of all people in society and pushes for acceptance and education of women's issues and issues of equality being discussed and advocated for in universities, academic journals, and wider public spheres.

Sparking the Second Wave

After the return to domestic life following World War II, women were growing restless. They had many modern conveniences—appliances that made taking care of home and family easier, husbands to manage their finances, and automobiles to take them to new areas of the country. However, this type of life wasn't fulfilling for every woman. Some wanted more from life and began looking for new, meaningful opportunities to spend their time.

In the late 1950s, Betty Friedan, a housewife who had earned a degree in psychology in 1942, also began to question her role in society. She thought to explore other women's feelings on childcare and homemaking. Her research focused on middle- and upper-class women in the suburbs, her former classmates. She circulated a questionnaire, and the results surprised her. She found that many of the women she had graduated with were suffering from a "problem that has no name." These women, who had suburban homes, husbands, children, and leisure time, felt unhappy and unfulfilled in their lives as homemakers. Friedan concluded that they were craving something more than just a home and family; they wanted something of their own.

Friedan built a case for women breaking out of traditional roles of wife and mother. Her research culminated in the writing and publication of *The Feminine Mystique*, published in 1963, a work which ignited **second-wave feminism**.

Along with *The Feminine Mystique*, another development that helped the second-wave feminists gain momentum was the introduction of the birth control pill. For the first time, women who wanted to focus on having a career did not have to worry about an unplanned pregnancy interrupting their development in the workforce. While birth control was illegal in many states and other states only allowed married women to use oral contraceptives, in 1972, the Supreme Court legalized contraceptives for all women, even if they were unmarried.

Working for Equality

In the 1960s, women began to protest unequal treatment in society and advocate for themselves. One such protest, the Women's Strike for Equality, gained national coverage when twenty thousand women gathered on Fifth Avenue in New York City to protest pay inequality, social inequality, and political exclusion. Other notable protests include the 1968 Miss America Pageant, where women protested outside the venue, insisting that such an institution promoted the social belief that women were only valuable for their looks.

By fighting against objectification and marginalization, the movement made several steps toward women's equality. They brought issues of rape and marital rape to the American public; helped pass legislation preventing credit agencies from discriminating on the basis of sex and employers from firing pregnant employees; helped grant women, infants, and children food assistance; opened the first battered women's shelters; and started several women's publications devoted to intelligent debate on women's issues.

In 1963, the Equal Pay Act was introduced into US legislation, making it illegal to pay women less than men for doing the same job, something that Susan B. Anthony had criticized nearly one hundred years earlier. While this was small progress, it excluded executive and administrative positions, which were typically only held by men, and "professionals." "Professionals" was a broad enough term to justify continued pay inequality until the text was revised in 1972.

The feminist art movement of the 1960s and 1970s inspired more women than ever to participate in visual arts. By using conceptual and interactive images alongside more traditional mediums, the feminist artists sought to bring the continued struggle for equality of women to the forefront of the American consciousness. Some feminist artists combined performance and visual art with activism by staging large-scale exhibitions that brought issues like violence against women to mind. Notable feminist artists during this time were Judy Chicago, Suzanne Lacy, Leslie Labowitz, and Cindy Sherman. Through exaggerated or hyper-realistic self portraits and portraits of those suffering around them, these women challenged people to think outside their comfort zones and examine the many social issues that plagued the country.

During the Vietnam War, many people fought against the war by staging marches and other nonviolent protests.

Hippies and Flower Power

Like the flappers of the 1920s, the young women of the 1960s and 1970s were ready to break with their mother's conservative culture. "Hippies," a word derived from "hipster," which had been used to describe the 1950s jazz and beatnik counterculture, were a subculture concerned with promoting peace and tolerance, returning to nature, artistic and sexual expression, and recreational drug use.

Hippies advocated for peaceful protest. They organized many sit-ins, strikes, and marches to promote civil rights or demand an end to war. Many women and men in the hippie movement broke from traditional parenting roles, taking a more equal share of responsibility in household chores and childrearing.

Hippie subcultures gave women the power to be individuals, but also offered a different ideal of domesticity for women who felt that the previous generation had become too consumerist and lost sight of what was truly important in life.

Civil Rights

Along with women's fight for liberation, several other groups formed to protest oppression. "Black pride," "brown pride," and "gay pride" all became terms used to describe civil rights protests in the 1960s and 1970s. As equality movements grew, many women became involved in trying to change their circumstances—not just as women, but as members of other groups.

Angela Davis and Assata Shakur both became prominent figures in the radical Black Panthers movement. The Black Panthers believed in gaining equality by any means necessary, which sometimes meant resorting to violence. While police forces often targeted them and many Black Panthers were arrested, they opened health clinics and daycares in impoverished areas to help pull African American people out

Assata Shakur and other Black Panthers were arrested for their radical protests against racism.

of poverty caused by institutionalized racism. Many women in the group were writers, public speakers, and activists who brought public attention to the plight of black women in the United States and called out racial inequality, and even chauvinism within the Black Panther Party.

In the 1960s and 1970s, being lesbian, gay, or bisexual (LGB) was not just considered a social evil, but it was also illegal in some states. Employers routinely fired employees based on their sexual orientation. Many people were prohibited from joining the military or holding federal jobs if they displayed "homosexual behavior," a term so vague as to apply to almost anything. Some psychoanalysts at the time believed that different sexual orientations were a form of mental illness, and many homosexual people received shock therapy and conversion therapy as a result. Building off the women's rights and equality movements, the LGB community started advocating for their own rights. During this time, Elaine Noble became the first openly lesbian woman to serve on a state legislature in 1974. She served two terms.

Third-Wave Feminism

One of the many critiques of the first and second waves of feminism was that middle-class white women seemed to be the focus of the movements. People of other races, people who did not conform to traditional gender roles, single mothers, or poor women were often left out.

Third-wave feminism focused much more on the intersectionality of women's issues with other areas of their lives. Major issues included race, class, ethnicity, economics, and gender identity. They sought to influence and reclaim concepts, words, ideas, and symbols that held women to traditional roles.

Today, third-wave feminism focuses on many aspects of inequality that arise in society in more insidious ways: by looking at stereotypes in television and movies that reinforce negative opinions about women, examining how race and culture intermingle to produce specific hurdles for women of color, and how language shapes the way we react to situations. One example of this was a 1980s campaign by the anonymous artists the Guerrilla Girls, who embody many of the ideals of third-wave feminism. The Guerilla Girls, examining the ways women were represented in museums, art shows, and artwork, produced flyers that asked, "Do Women Have to Be Nude to Get Into the Met Museum?" The bold statement and flashy graphics pulled people in, and the facts displayed at the bottom of the flyer explained their purpose. By using tactics like these, many third-wave feminist groups reach a large audience with their critiques of societal inequality.

Women in Politics

One of the major changes that grew out of the suffragette movement was an increase in the number of women who participate in politics. Despite anti-suffrage claims that

THE LEAGUE OF WOMEN VOTERS TODAY

After passage of the Nineteenth Amendment, NAWSA president Carrie Chapman Catt turned the NAWSA into the League of Women Voters. The institution provided education on governmental candidates and referenda on the ballot, engaged women in discussions around politics and how politics affected their everyday lives, and advocated for women to vote. Today, they have leagues in every state, as well as in the Virgin Islands and Hong Kong.

In 1918, they were one of the groups that lobbied most fervently for the creation of the League of Nations, and today they continue to support many progressive policies. Though they consider themselves nonpartisan, they support clean air and water acts, universal health care, and abolishing the death penalty.

They continue to run campaigns related to voter issues. In the 1990s, the League of Women Voters fought for the National Voter Registration Act, which allowed ease of access to obtaining and maintaining voter registration. The bill, popularly called "the Motor Voter Act," was passed in 1993. One of the provisions of the act was that all people applying for or renewing a driver's license can register to vote at the same time.

women had temperaments too frail to allow them to actively engage with politics in the 1800s, women have shown that they have the leadership skills not just to cast a ballot, but to run for office.

Jeanette Rankin was elected to office for the first time prior to the ratification of the Nineteenth Amendment, which meant that when she ran, most women in the country would not have been able to cast a vote for her. Before being elected to office, she spent time working on several suffrage campaigns in the Western states. She ran for Congress in Montana, promoting herself through a campaign of pacifism, working toward nationwide suffrage, and social reform. She came in second, becoming the first woman elected to Congress in 1916.

After Jeanette Rankin, many more women would be elected to the House and Senate. The percentage of female electees that serve each institution have continued to steadily increase, with the biggest gains in the early 1990s, when the number of women nearly doubled in both the House and the Senate. The percentage of women in both the House and the Senate is currently about 20 percent, and only five states have never elected a woman to the House of Representatives.

The first woman to ever run for president in the United States was Victoria Woodhull in 1872, as the Equal Rights Party candidate. She did not expect to win, but she did want to drive home the point that women were capable of running for office, so they should surely be capable of voting. She also wanted to show the hypocrisy of making it illegal for women to vote but not to run for office.

Belva Lockwood ran on the National Equal Rights Party ticket in 1884 and 1888, and Southern suffragette Laura Clay was put forth as a candidate at the Democratic National Convention in 1920, though not a single constituent voted for her candidacy. Margaret Chase Smith was the first woman

Victoria Woodhull was the first woman to run for president in the history of the United States.

to serve in both the House and the Senate, and in 1964 was the first woman to run in a primary election for a major party in the United States.

Charlene Mitchell was the first African American woman on the ballot in a presidential election in 1968, even though she ran for the Communist Party, which was so small she only appeared on the ballot in two states. Four years later, Shirley Chisholm would be the first African American primary candidate of a major party when she appeared on the Democratic primary ballot. In 1972, in addition to Shirley Chisholm, two other women ran in the Democratic primary: prominent feminist leaders Bella Abzug and Patsy Takemoto Mink.

There have only been three women ever to run on major party tickets in the presidential election in the United States. In 1984, Geraldine Ferraro made history when she became the first female vice presidential candidate of a major party, and the first Italian American to appear on the presidential ballot. She and her running mate, Democrat Walter Mondale, would lose, but she would later go on to serve as the United States Ambassador to the United Nations Commission on Human Rights in the mid 1990s. Sarah Palin, who ran as the Republican vice presidential candidate alongside John McCain in 2008, became the second woman to ever run for that office for one of the two major parties. In 2016, Hillary Clinton became the first woman to run as a presidential candidate on a major party line when she became the Democratic Party candidate.

HILLARY RODHAM CLINTON

When Hillary Rodham Clinton was growing up in a middle-class suburb of Chicago, no one would have ever dreamed she, or any woman, would run for president in their lifetimes. As a student, Clinton attended Wellesley College, where she became involved with social and political activism. Her interaction with civil rights showed her the many inequalities that existed

Hillary Rodham Clinton waves to crowds on November 8, 2016, one day before the 2016 presidential election.

in American life. She enrolled in Yale Law School in 1969, and was one of just twenty-seven women in her graduating class in 1973.

While attending law school, Hillary Rodham took a job helping migrant farmworkers one summer. There she saw firsthand how little access migrant workers had to education and health care. It was during this time that her focus shifted to children's rights. Following her law school graduation, she took a job for the Children's Defense Fund, and later would co-found the Arkansas Advocates for Children and Families.

As First Lady of Arkansas in the 1990s, she worked to improve education and health care for children in her state. As First Lady of the United States, she focused on health care reform on a national level, helping to pass the Children's Health Insurance Program (CHIP), which provided insurance to thousands of children who had previously not had coverage.

She went on to serve as the first female senator from New York State, and then as Secretary of State under President Barack Obama. In 2016 she was the Democratic candidate for president, but despite winning the popular vote, she lost the election to Republican candidate Donald Trump.

Nevertheless, Clinton's personal and political efforts have contributed to countless new opportunities for children and prove that women can make a difference in politics.

Women Today, and the Legacy of Suffrage

The world as we know it today would look much different without the contributions that the suffragettes made. Not only do we continue to admire the women who fought for the right to vote in the first wave of feminism, but these women are commemorated on US postal stamps and in speeches promoting human rights today.

The suffragettes were not given anything; they fought hard for enfranchisement. They did not only win the right to vote for half of the American population; they provided the right for women to represent their own interests in politics. This, in turn, gave second-wave feminists new avenues to pursue equality. By voting, campaigning in politics, and using several of the civil disobedience tactics the suffragettes used, second-wave feminists helped pass legislation that brought women closer to pay equality, raised awareness of the objectification of women, and forged new roads for women in the United States.

While the first and second waves are often criticized for ignoring the rights of women of color and LGBT women, their efforts allowed women to speak up for all wrongs in society, as they have in the third wave. They gave women the right to speak publicly about their lives and lobby effectively for equality even today.

Without the suffragettes, women may not have experienced many of the rights they have today. There do still remain barriers to break before becoming truly equal, but the groundwork for that process was laid long ago by women willing to sacrifice for us to have a better future.

abolitionist movement A reform movement to end slavery.

activists People who fight against injustice, usually by lobbying for a specific cause.

ballot The form used to cast a vote.

civil disobedience An act or acts that defy the law in order to bring awareness to a social issue.

conscription Mandated military service, usually via a draft.

Declaration of Sentiments A list of demands for women's equality written by Elizabeth Cady Stanton that included suffrage.

draft A forced recruitment of military personnel.

electorate The group of people who are eligible to vote under the law of a state or nation.

enfranchisement Having full citizenship, including voting rights.

first-wave feminists Women who participated in the suffrage movement of the late nineteenth and early twentieth centuries.

flapper A 1920s woman characterized by bobbed hair, shorter skirt lengths, jazz music and dancing, and attending speakeasies.

hunger strike Refusing food in order to gain sympathy for a cause.

laisser-faire An attitude of noninvolvement.

muckraker Investigative journalist who exposed corruption and deceit in big business and government.

New Deal A series of reforms instituted by President Franklin D. Roosevelt to lift the country out of the Great Depression. They included public works projects and social welfare programs.

New Woman A woman who breaks from traditional roles of womanhood. She is educated, career-oriented, and independent.

Night of Terror A night in the Occoquan Workhouse when female suffrage prisoners were physically beaten in an attempt to get them to stop protesting and picketing.

Nineteenth Amendment The amendment to the US Constitution that granted women the right to vote.

pacifist A person who believes that it is better to abstain from violence and war than participate in it.

petition A proposal that is passed around to get signatures to show legislators that the public supports or does not support a certain idea.

political party A group of people who hold similar social and legislative beliefs and work together to elect new legislators. The two major political parties in the United States are the Republican and Democratic Parties.

Progressive Movement A period dedicated to modernizing American life and ending political corruption between 1890 and 1920. Also called the Progressive Era.

prohibition An era in the United States between 1920 and 1933 during which time the production and sale of alcoholic beverages were banned.

Quaker A member of the Society of Friends religion who believes that each person is equal and carries God within themselves as an inner light.

radical An idea or behavior that is far outside the current societal norm.

ratification The process by which a proposal becomes a law.

second-wave feminism The period of feminism between the 1960s and the 1980s during which women pressed for equal pay, political involvement, family planning, and liberation.

settlement house A house that is occupied by middle- or upper-class white women in a poor area, dedicated to helping people in poverty empower and uplift themselves.

suffrage The idea that women can vote.

suffragette The name given to a woman who fights for suffrage.

Taylorism The application of science, logic, and efficiency to maximize workplace productivity.

temperance movement The movement to ban alcohol and educate people on the dangers of liquor.

third-wave feminism The current era in feminism, concerned with giving a voice to women of all races, classes, and sexual orientations.

CHRONOLOGY

1833 Oberlin College becomes the first to admit women and African Americans.

1848 Seneca Falls Convention is held, and the Declaration of Sentiments is presented.

1850 First National Women's Rights Convention.

1851 Bloomer craze. Sojourner Truth delivers her "Ain't I A Woman" speech in Akron, Ohio.

1852 *Uncle Tom's Cabin is* published.

1861 Civil War begins.

1863 The Women's National Loyal League is formed.

1865 Civil War ends.

1866 American Equal Rights Association (AERA) forms. Vassar College forms its first all-women baseball teams.

1869 The National Woman Suffrage Association is formed by Susan B. Anthony and Elizabeth Cady Stanton. The American Woman Suffrage Association is formed by Lucy Stone, Henry Blackwell, and Julia Ward Howe.

1870 Wyoming grants universal suffrage.

1871 The Anti Suffrage Society is formed.

1872 Susan B. Anthony registers to vote, and votes. She is arrested. Victoria Woodhull runs for president.

1874 *Minor v. Happersett.* Women's Christian Temperance Union is founded.

1889 Hull House is opened by Jane Addams and Ellen Starr in Chicago.

1890 The General Federation of Women's Clubs is founded. National American Woman Suffrage Association is created by combining the AWSA and the NWSA. Bicycles become popular with American women. The Progressive Era begins.

1900 Olympics allow women to compete in the Paris games. Carrie Chapman Catt becomes the president of the NAWSA.

1911 Triangle Shirtwaist Factory Fire. The National Association Opposed to Woman Suffrage is formed.

1913 Woodrow Wilson becomes president. The day before his inauguration, suffragettes stage the Woman Suffrage Parade of 1913.

1914 World War I begins.

1916 Jeanette Rankin elected to the US House of Representatives. The National Woman's Party is founded by Alice Paul.

1917 America joins World War I. The Silent Sentinels begin picketing the White House.

November 14, 1917 "The Night of Terror" in Occoquan Workhouse.

1918 World War I ends.

1920 Nineteenth Amendment is ratified. The NAWSA becomes the League of Women Voters.

Books

Bausum, Ann. *With Courage and Cloth: Winning the Fight for a Woman's Right to Vote*. Washington, DC: National Geographic, 2004.

Collins, Gail. *America's Women: 400 Years of Dolls, Drudges, Helpmates, and Heroines*. New York: Morrow, 2003.

Cooper, Illene. *A Woman in the House (and Senate): How Women Came to the United States Congress, Broke down Barriers, and Changed the Country*. New York: Abrams Books for Young Readers, 2014.

Drinkwater, Catherine. *Suffragette: The Diary of Dollie Baxter*. New York: Scholastic, 2003.

Hollihan, Kerry Logan. *Rightfully Ours: How Women Won the Vote: 21 Activities*. Chicago, IL: Chicago Review Press, 2012.

Macy, Sue, et al. *Wheels of Change: How Women Rode the Bicycle to Freedom (with a Few Flat Tires along the Way)*. Washington, DC: National Geographic, 2011.

Myers, Walter Dean. *Ida B. Wells: Let the Truth Be Told*. New York: Amistad/HarperCollins, 2008.

Thimmesh, Catherine, and Douglas B Jones. *Madam President*. Boston, MA: Houghton Mifflin, 2004.

Websites

Crusade for the Vote

http://www.crusadeforthevote.org

The National Women's History Museum presents the history of suffrage in the United States and beyond.

Not for Ourselves Alone

http://www.pbs.org/stantonanthony

This website offers videos, documents, and discussions detailing the history of the women's movement.

Women Suffrage and the Nineteenth Amendment

https://www.archives.gov/education/lessons/woman-suffrage

This website gives a look at the source documents of the women's movement in the United States.

Videos

Crash Course US History: Women's Suffrage

https://www.youtube.com/watch?v=HGEMscZE5dY

Bestselling author John Green offers an overview of the important events in the suffrage movement with comedic commentary.

History Channel: The Fight for Women's Suffrage

http://www.history.com/topics/womens-history/the-fight-for-womens-suffrage/videos

Visit the History Channel's collected video documentation of women making history.

Makers: Women who Make America

http://www.pbs.org/show/makers-women-who-make-america/

This PBS miniseries explores the history of women breaking through barriers to achieve new heights.

"A Kansas Woman Runs for Congress," *The Independent*. Archive.org. Accessed October 19, 2016. https://archive.org/stream/independen79v80newy#page/n71/mode/1up.

Bly, Nellie. "Champion of Her Sex," *New York Sunday World*, February 2, 1896, p. 10.

Collins, Gail. *America's Women: 400 Years of Dolls, Drudges, Helpmates, and Heroines*. New York: Morrow, 2003.

Cooney, Robert. "Enduring Significance of the American Woman Suffrage Movement." Women's Studies Reading Room. Accessed November 21, 2016. http://mith.umd.edu/WomensStudies/ReadingRoom/History/Vote/enduring-significance.html.

Du Bois, W. E. B. "Woman suffrage." *Crisis* 11 (1915): 29–30.

"The First New Woman," *The Washington Post*, August 11, 1895, p. 20.

Freeman, Jo. "From Suffrage to Women's Liberation: Feminism in 20th Century America." Published in *Women: A Feminist*

Perspective. Mountain View, CA: Mayfield, 5th edition, 1995, pp. 509-28.

Friedan, Betty. *The Feminine Mystique.* New York: W.W. Norton, 1963.

Gaughen, Shasta. *Women's Rights.* San Diego, CA: Greenhaven Press, 2003.

hooks, bell. *Feminist Theory: From Margin to Center.* Cambridge, MA: South End Press, 2000.

Irwin, Inez Hayes. *The Story of Alice Paul and the National Woman's Party.* Fairfax, VA: Denlinger's Publishers, 1920; reprint 1977.

Nardo, Dan. *The Women's Movement.* New York: Lucent Books, 2011.

Rossi, Ann. *Created Equal: Women Campaign for the Right to Vote.* Washington, DC: National Geographic Society, 2005.

Stanton, Elizabeth Cady. "Declaration of sentiments and resolutions." 1848.

"Wyoming Constitution." Wyoming Constitution. Accessed October 15, 2016. http://www.uwyo.edu/robertshistory/ wyoming_constitution_full_text.htm.

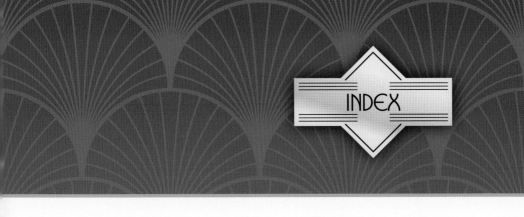

INDEX

Page numbers in **boldface** are illustrations. Entries in **boldface** are glossary terms.

Paul, Alice, 49–53, 55, 61, 65, **82**, 85–86

petition, 13, 29, 43, 45, 47, 50

political party, 23

politics, 7, 13, 22, 24, 27, 37, 58, 66, 90, 105–107, 111–112

Progressive Movement/Era, 26, 28, 32, 49, 64

prohibition, 21, 23–24, 54

Quaker, 22, 42–43, 45

radical, 24, 50, 53, 103

ratification, 24, 33, 58, 81–82, 86–87, 107

Roosevelt, Eleanor, 89–90

Rosie the Riveter, 95, **95**

salons, 37

Schlafly, Phyllis, 85–86

second-wave feminism, **96**, 99, 112

Seneca Falls Convention, 38, 40

settlement house, 62

Stanton, Elizabeth Cady, 13, 20, **36**, 37–40, **44**, 45–47, 49

Stone, Lucy, 38, 47–49, 63

Stowe, Harriet Beecher, 74

suffrage, 16–17, 19–20, 22–23, 28, 34, 37, 39, 43, 48–54, 56–58, 61, 63, 65, 67–68, 70, 73, 80, 89, 107, 112

suffragette, 44, 50–53, 56–57, 61–63, 67, 69–70, 80, 97–98, 105, 108, 112

Tarbell, Ida, 27

Taylorism, 27

Temperance Movement, 19, 21, 26

third-wave feminism, 104–105

Thirteenth Amendment, 13

Triangle Shirtwaist Factory Fire, 30, **31**

Truth, Sojourner, 20, 41

Wells, Ida B., 28, **64**, 65

Willard, Frances, 24

Wilson, President Woodrow, 16–17, 50, 57, 80–81

Women Air Force Service Pilots (WASPs), 93

Women's Army Corps (WAC), **92**, 93

Women's Christian Temperance Union (WCTU), 23–24

Women's Loyal National League (WLNL), 13

Woodhull, Victoria, 107, **108**

Meghan Cooper is a teacher and writer living in Brooklyn, New York, with her husband and children.